For those who encouraged (sometimes without noticing) me to find my voice. This is my introduction to the world and I have all of you to thank for it.

<u>A Letter</u>

Dear Mrs. R,

I know you insist on me calling you Susie since so many years have passed but I can't help but feel it wouldn't be right. We always joke about me being your "first child", maybe I was the first kid you cared for. You were nearly twenty-eight when you taught me, I was just ten and it was your second year of teaching. I will never forget the light blue ribbed sweater you wore; I think it was the first day of school. I had never seen anything look so elegant. I know you think its flattery, but you don't look any different than that first day. It was the first time in my life I met a woman, other than my mom, that I looked up to. Everything you did was magic. The way you printed the date on the chalk board to the way you dressed, I wanted to be you. A real person, not someone on T.V., you. Things were so hard for me, harder then they should've been. When I look back now, I understand why I acted the way I did. Why I couldn't manage my anger, why I had such a problem with peers. Though miniscule, I'm so happy that that small problem, that peer-to-peer issue that I can't even remember, brought me to you afterschool. I remember how open you were. It was the first time in my life an adult told me (along with the rest of the class) that their door was open. That whatever was going on, an adult cared and would listen. I don't know what you saw in me. I have no idea how you knew it was more than that small issue, but you did, and you listened. You listened for two years until I walked across that stage and graduated elementary school. A part of me thought that's where your obligation ended. I knew I would see you again because my siblings were still there, but you couldn't possibly care about me. I was wrong. You were there when I got my first job, when I decided to move out for the first time, when I got my heart broken, when I thought I would never get out of that three block radius, you were there. You were there to offer advice; you were the first adult to tell me you're proud of me. You were the one who said my name would "look good on the cover of a book." You were the one that taught me I didn't have to be special to be loved. You now have two, almost grown kids of your own and if you've shown them even a sliver of the care and devotion you've shown to me, I'm sure they're doing just fine.

Mrs. R, you're one of the reasons I'm still alive. If you didn't open your door and your heart to me twenty-one years ago, if you didn't teach me I have a voice, if you didn't believe in me, if you didn't love your profession, I would not be here today. You saw something in me that I didn't see in myself. You taught me I was worthy of education and a better life. Twenty-one years later you're still someone I look up to, you're still my mentor, and now you're one of my best friends. There are no words that can describe my gratitude but will try with two.

THANK YOU.

Love always,

Your first child,

Michelle.

<u>March Break</u>

I've been waiting since Christmas to hear the bell ring today. When the bell rings at 3:30pm my dad will be back from working abroad and I'll have the entire week to play Crash Bandicoot on our new Playstation, and with dad home, I don't have to take care of my little brother when my mom's at work! Just twenty more minutes until I'm out of here, I can't wait! I'm going to listen to my CD's on the big stereo all week! When that bell rings it will be only thirty-six days until my birthday, and I'll be thirteen. I can't believe I'll be thirteen, that's crazy. I hope I get to order from Colombia House for my birthday. Usually that's only in September and I would have to split it with my sister, but I have a good feeling about it. Just ten more minutes until the bell! I don't even have to walk home today. I hope we get Pizza Hut tonight and I can stay up to watch Breaker High. Three minutes until the bell! Okay, let me get Justin's number in case we have to work on our project together.

Man this sucks. My tummy hurts on the first night of March Break. Maybe it was the KFC. I don't even want to be on MSN anymore, I think I'll turn on the radio and go to sleep.

Aw man, I can hear my sister downstairs, I hope she's not playing first. I'm going to get some frosted flakes and kick her off.

My tummy still feels weird, maybe it's because I've been sitting too long. I'll try and go to the bathroom. What was that? Did I pee myself? Oh no. Oh no, no, no. "Moooommmmmmmmmmm".

"Scott, guess what?! She got her period!"

<u>The Librarian</u>

I slinked into the library just before the lunch bell in hopes Mrs. G didn't see me. I was late, again. Although I loved being in school and loved learning, I hated my situation. My dad moved back in and all of a sudden rules have changed and my mom doesn't trust me anymore. My boyfriend smushed my face against the bed last night because of an argument and I have a swollen cheek. That's probably the main reason I don't want Mrs. G to see me. I'm tired of lying. I'm late because I didn't have a place to stay since my boyfriend and I fought. It's just embarrassing. I'm lucky I even got here this morning. I snuck onto the bus with my wrinkled uniform. I know uniforms are supposed to make us feel uniform, but I can't help but feel like I still don't belong here. I must've been reading too loudly because Mrs. G came around the corner with her mild limp, looked at me above her glasses and simply said "lunch time, will you go for a walk?". I knew what that meant. She always asked me to walk across the street to the Chinese food place to pick up some lunch for her. "Lemon Chicken with fried rice as usual?" I asked. "You got it." Mrs. G replied enthusiastically. She handed me a twenty-dollar bill "get whatever you want, too." Every day I politely declined and every day she always insisted because I was *doing her a favour*. Sometimes when I came back in, she wouldn't even eat it. I'm sure she just wanted to buy me a meal. When I came back in, Mrs. G noticed my face. She gently touched my unbruised cheek to turn my head and take a closer look. "What happened?". As I barely opened my sore mouth to take a bite of my fried rice, I responded with "probably just slept weird". I've always been a bad liar. I don't know if it

was the stain from two days ago on my collar, if I

smelled, or if it was the bruise on my face, but Mrs. G

wasn't buying it. "Where did you sleep?". I was out

of lies, I could barely see out of my broken glasses

and now my vision was completely impaired as the

tears started to roll down my uneven cheeks.

"Nowhere" I whimpered before I started blubbering

all over the returned book pile in the office. My

parents kicked me out for breaking curfew to *"teach

me a lesson"*, my boyfriend wasn't being great and

I've run out of stories and friends to crash with.

Over the next three weeks Mrs. G took control over

my situation. Every spare moment she had, she

dedicated time to try and get me back on track. She

organized a schedule with my teachers where I could

work independently in the library under her

supervision. After school she even took me to the optometrist. She researched social services available to me and helped me get an apartment. She even gave me an unused bed from her house.

The following weeks were tough. I continued to see my abusive boyfriend, but I reconciled with my mom and she let me see my brother and sister again. Although things were on the up and up, it didn't stay that way. I eventually left school without a goodbye. Maybe it was sheer embarrassment then, but there's not a day that goes by where I don't say thank you to the universe for my Librarian. Without you I wouldn't have found hope, words, or dreams.

Mrs. G, I'm sorry. Your help didn't die in vain. It's the reason for all the stamps in my passport and all the words on this page.

<u>I Lov(ed) You</u>

I loved you. I mean I really loved you. The kind of love people sing about. I loved you from the tips of my toes to the ends of my hair. I loved everything about you. Your laugh, your smile, your touch. I loved the way we meshed. I loved your smell and the way you made your bed. I loved the way you typed and how you said you loved me. I loved that we were young and you waited for me. I loved that you went down on me first. I loved the way we laid together and you would hold me all night. I loved he way you couldn't handle just being my friend the first time we broke up. I loved that you loved my baby brother. I loved that you loved my passion for basketball. I loved that you loved my hair the way it is. I loved you. I really loved you. I loved you when you pressed my head against the pillow. I loved you when you ripped my uniform off although I yelled no. I loved you when you pulled my hair and told me to "shut up". I loved you when I hollered with tears in my eyes, "I'm not ready!" I loved you when I begged "…not like this". I loved you when you violently entered me, and my body went limp. I loved you when you finished and cried and said sorry. I believed you. I loved you when I missed my period. I loved you when you said, "it's your decision". I loved you when you told me you couldn't come to the appointment. I loved you when I laid down and heard the machine start. I loved you when I came back and you hugged me. I loved you when bathed me and watched me cry. I loved you over and over again. I loved you until I couldn't anymore.

<u>L.A.</u>

There was a sense of melancholy when I landed. I didn't know what to expect but somehow, I was sad about it. You left so suddenly and we hadn't seen each other since we were kids. When I got to the house, you looked the same, just skinner. Your brothers were so grown and although it had been years, it was like no time had passed. I saw your new life. Trying to be like your eldest brother. Being where you shouldn't. We spent many innocent nights laying together. Talking about our dreams, how the neighbourhood has changed since you've left. I met your friends, saw where you lived, it was like watching a movie in slow motion. You changed; LA changed you. From the way you spoke to how you perceived your future. On my last day we made plans to meet on the east coast because you couldn't cross

the border. We talked about a magical new year eve
in New York city. I promised to call when I got
home. You promised to stop being where you
shouldn't. I called and called but my calls went
unanswered. August came around and I called to wish
you a happy birthday, one of your younger brothers
spoke for you saying thank you. New Year's Eve
came and all I could think of was you. I called and
got another brother and another excuse. Finally, your
mom picked up the phone and told me. My heart
dropped to my stomach. Three strike rule, in jail. I
was so angry. Why? This isn't you. I wrote your
eldest brother who was also locked up. Angry at him
for getting you into this shit. I wrote you. It took
some time, but you wrote me back. I was there for
you. Phone calls, photos, letters, I was there. Trips to
L.A., buying your younger brothers back to school

clothes at the swap meet. Hanging with your mom. I was there.

You got out. I had no idea, found out and booked the first plane I could to see you and your brother. You chose a ski trip over me. I was hurt but distracted by L.A.'s bright lights. I grew close to your older brother, he told me you'd come around.

Year after Year passed and I tried keeping in touch. I messaged, called, flew to L.A. casually a few times. On my way to Australia I stopped in and you actually responded, seemed happy to see me, you sounded good on the phone. I was jet lagged and tired, but I showed up to the suggested place to meet on Hollywood. I waited an hour for you and when you finally showed up, you were distracted. You looked like you hadn't slept in three days and you were bouncing off the walls. You introduced me to about ten people in one minute, you ordered a shot of liquor at two in the afternoon and said you had to run somewhere, and I should wait with "Tony". You didn't come back. After that I didn't try anymore. No more flights, calls, letters.

In 2016 my mom turned sixty and I surprised her with a trip. Our moms were close, and eighteen years had passed since they were reunited. It was my last straw. Everyone showed up, every brother and you were MIA. No explanation. I thought if not for me, at least for my mom.

I don't know what I expected when I got on that plane. I don't know what I expected when you got out of jail. I guess I just expected a friend. I heard you went through a hard time, I heard it wasn't easy. I tried to be there, but L.A. is now too far gone.

My Body

"I can't do it like this" he said standing there butt ass naked standing at attention. "I think you're sexy but clearly you're uncomfortable so call me when you find yourself sexy." Dumbfounded, I lay there in the dark with my ripped pajama shirt and the blanket covering my exposed legs. I couldn't believe it.

"How did it go?!" Deon screamed as I walked into work. "It didn't" I smugly responded. "What happened?!" she exclaimed "…well" I start. Do I tell her? I thought to myself. A part of me was embarrassed. "He left as soon as it started getting hot and heavy." I continued. Surprised, Deon looked at me with her head to side as she usually does and asked "What?! Why??" "…well" I stumble again. "Spill it bitch." She firmly ordered. I told her exactly what happened. She immediately laughed hysterically and agreed with Mr. Man "OF COURSE!" she exclaimed "look at you, you have the best ass! You're hot, why the hell are you wearing a bummy shirt to sleep with someone?!" Before continuing, she grabbed my shoulder and looked me dead in the eyes "get yourself together and when you're ready, call him back!".

A few weeks passed but eventually I messaged him. I told him to come over. He was hesitant but I promised to meet him at the door in nothing but a trench coat and heels. As soon as I opened the door, we did what we should've done weeks ago and in that moment, I fell in love with my body.

AIR

I can't live without you, you make my ears pop,

I hate what you do to my world that was once without

your toxicity,

You are the reason I strive, how I move and survive,

Every cent earned goes to my captivity in your body,

I can't wait to be inside you again.

<u>My Body Part II</u>

Twenty-nine years old and I've never masturbated.
I've probably orgasmed twice in my life. No one ever
taught me what I was supposed to do. I knew
somethings that made me feel good, but I never 'let
go'. It was a week before my thirtieth and I refused to
go into my thirtieth year unpleased and waiting for
someone else to help me find my pleasure. So, I
dedicated an afternoon to 'letting go'. I thought about
past lovers while massaging my lotus flower. After
what seemed like forever, there it was. Fireworks
inside. My legs shook, my sheets under me wet, I
finally let go. My first immediate thought?

WHY HAVEN'T I DONE THIS BEFORE?!

FUN

We were fun

Strangers through text

A vision once met

Your touch was familiar

I yearned for it once gone

Your gaze unlike your words remained long

Different languages now

Time has run out slowly

We run after it to remember

We were fun

Lovers lost in time

Distance between us

A New Day

By the emerald hills,

Through the blowing wind,

Battling the waves along the shore,

In between broken clouds,

The sun shined on a Sunday morning,

You welcomed me.

About The Author

Michelle Spences-Lee is a Canadian born writer and travel enthusiast. She attended The University of Toronto before embarking on her journey, fulfilling her dream of travelling full-time. She has currently visited fifty-nine countries and counting. She presently resides in Dublin, Ireland for the short-term. This is Michelle's first independent publication. She has been featured in *Tilde~ A Literary Journal 4* in 2019 and has two anticipated novels, *Things I've Never Said Aloud* and *Livin' La Vida Broka: The Essential Travel Guide to Travelling While Broke* to be released in 2020. You can find Michelle on Instagram @thewordmichelle.

Coming of Age, A Little Late
Originally published April 16th 2018 Catapult
Magazine

Coming of Age, A Little Late

A personal essay

In Film, "coming of age" usually happens in high school. You have a character who develops over the course of two hours and recognizes at sixteen who they are and what they want to be. For a select few this may be true. Maybe people actually become decent human beings and incredibly secure at a young age. For me that was definitely not the case. I was a physically and emotionally abused teen in an unhealthy relationship with myself. I was awkward, chubby, tall, gap toothed, and hated myself. I hated myself physically, I hated how my brain worked, and I hated where I was in life. I was constantly reminded by media and society that if I didn't know who I was then, I'll never know. I can't pinpoint which exact life event changed me, changed my whole perspective but what I can note is the time it took. For the past ten years I've been working up until my coming of age.

Growing up awkwardly in a city that didn't have many options or alternate views in the 90's and early 00's wasn't easy. Clothes didn't fit, magazines and media didn't offer images of anyone that looked like me, my own mother didn't have a healthy view of herself, let alone her daughters. It was a difficult time. It wasn't until 2010 after recollecting on family health issues and educating myself that my physical evolution began. I'm still tall, thick, gap toothed, and a bit awkward – don't get me wrong, but my health took a front seat and was the entry to my self-love journey (coming of age). I learned that I consume for me and no one else, I taught myself that being healthy doesn't have a face or specific "look". It was the start of accepting myself and this didn't come in the beginning sequence of a film at fourteen, I was well into my twenties. I slowly, as well as the fashion industry, started to discover that I am not confined to the few "acceptable" plus size looks available to me. That I can feel sexy in an oversized Raptors jersey or a bodycon dress that shows my curves. I became aware that my "look" is desirable, I learned the difference in being fetishized and disrespected, and being courted and appreciated. Again, slowly (and I mean really slowly) I learned about pleasure in relation to my body. I embraced my feminism as a source of femininity and embellished my body without consequence from myself, how I saw fit.

My coming of age began with physical self-acceptance and it didn't start until age twenty-two, after years of abuse. Of course, it's an ongoing story that all of us fight, but I know, for me, until now I haven't looked or felt better physically. This is the part of the movie where the main character puts her/his glasses on after the classic straighten-hair-and-removes-glasses make over and realized s/he's just as beautiful without the makeover. My Dad use to, as we called it, preach to us. He would ramble on about how life is, what to expect within society and be brutally honest about who we were or how we were behaving at that point in time. I didn't understand then but what I do understand now is, to quote my dad as well as the fabulous RuPaul, "You must love yourself before loving someone else". This saying is so simple, yet **so true** and should be a life mantra for everyone. You cannot give what you do not have. This applies to everything and even after hearing it almost every day for over ten years from one of the only men in my life that loves me unconditionally, I didn't get it. Up until my mid-twenties I held onto unhealthy relationships including toxic friendships. I didn't realize how much this impacted my inner self (fancy psychology term I don't really understand on paper but understand emotionally). Growing up, and often now while living overseas, when I speak up about situations that aren't right, I was, and still am considered "sensitive". My parents tried the tough love thing on me when I would come home crying because a peer called me a "Fat bitch that shops at Bi-Way" (Toronto, specifically Scarborough people know what Bi-Way is) or when another classmate who pretended to not be my friend at recess even though we played together all weekend. These mild instances and many more intense encounters ultimately trained me to suppress my feelings, second guess myself, and intense anger issues that I didn't know how to control. I'm still working on it, but eventually I realized what my dad (and RuPaul) said is true. Charity begins at home (another one of my dad's favourites) and you have to start at the root. My over-promising just so people would like me, stopped. I started processing my feelings and realizing they are valid. Eventually I've become confident and vocal about what, how, and why I feel the way I do being able to articulate and accept my feelings. This self and honest reflection is the part of the film where the Paul Walker (RIP) type best friend is the worst person and the main character finally realizes it. This, in my personal experience has been the most important part of my coming of age experience because that best friend, you know the terrible one, is actually within yourself.

Society and media have a way of getting in your head. Subconsciously you can find yourself comparing your life to someone of another consequence. To go back to my dad's preaching, he would often tell us that "you can't compare yourself to others" and reminded us that though society might tell us one thing, that "there is no age limit". Personally, this has been the biggest struggle. Getting to my coming of age "late" comes with a lot of societal guilt and burden. I matured early and of course have been responsible however, coming into where I am now, I've made decisions for myself to live my best life that isn't societally popular. Up until twenty-six I did everything that was told to me societally. I studied, I finished, I worked great jobs, I paid my student loan every month, I tried to save, and I went on vacation once a year. Though I was doing everything "right" I wasn't feeling mentally present. This is the part in the movie that the main character realizes that s/he's too advanced for school. Think Lisa Simpson in every Simpsons episode. I made the choice to make a change and live my dream of travel and personal writing. It sounds easy as I write this down but breaking away from the societal norm and knowing that I won't own a house, or have a family by the time everyone else will or when we're told we're supposed to (or possibly ever) is hard because that's how we have been conditioned to think. My life overseas isn't glamourous. I work "basic" jobs and utilize every cent to travel the surrounding areas and save for the next big move (visas and moving countries is really expensive!). Thankfully throughout this process of coming to age, I've created an amazing support group of girlfriends, my family that includes my preach-y dad, my hilarious brother and sister, and my over supportive mother who constantly tells me she loves me and comments (and shares) every FaceBook post and picture with irrelevant emojis and improper spelling and punctuation (it's honestly the cutest thing). If it wasn't for my mental development and their support, I don't think I would get to this point of my journey.

Some people peak in high school, some in university or college, but for me it doesn't seem that I'm there yet, and that's okay! It took thirty years to get to this point of physical, emotional, and mental love and devotion and I know it will only get better. This is the part of the film that's unwritten but assumed. Think Breakfast Clubs last scene, don't you, forget about me.

---

[i] https://catapult.co/community/stories/coming-of-age-a-little-late